CITY OF PEARLS

CITY OF PEARLS

SHAM-E-ALI NAYEEM

POEMS

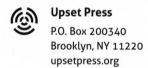

Upset Press
P.O. Box 200340
Brooklyn, NY 11220
upsetpress.org

Established in 2000, UpSet Press is an independent press based in Brooklyn. The original impetus of the press was to upset the status quo through literature. UpSet Press has expanded its mission to promote new work by new authors; the first works, or complete works, of established authors—placing a special emphasis on restoring to print new editions of exceptional texts; and first-time translations of works into English. Overall, UpSet Press endeavors to advance authors' innovative visions, and works that engender new directions in literature.

Front page cover design by Otura Mun and Wendy Lee
Interior design by Wendy Lee
Interior illustration by sab meynert / sabmeynert.com

Library of Congress Control Number: 2018958864
ISBN 978-1-937357-89-4
Second Printing
Printed in the United States of America

For Dad and Husayn

CONTENTS

If home is found on both sides of the globe,
home is of course here--
and always a missed land.

Agha Shahid Ali

CITY OF PEARLS

INVOCATION

My dad walks with me in the mornings.
The sun is new.
Even in the cold
I can feel him
in unknown spaces and collapse.

If I were sad he'd bring me fruit and water.
If I were scared he'd listen and offer counsel.
He would give me a poem.
He would tell me a joke.
I would know he was there.

I've never seen my dad cry
but I have seen him leave this world.
I felt him as a machine sang a flat note
parallel to a digital line on a screen.
I reached for his hand.

My dad walks with me in the mornings.
He taught me how to plant things.
He showed me how to herd sheep.
To pay attention to life force.
Listen to the earth.

He would tell me this is but a moment.
He would tell me you're a good mom.
He would show me maps in the sky and
how evergreens never lose their emerald.

He would read *Ayatul Kursi*
it would smell of safety and rose water.
He would say *Alif Lām Mīm*.
I would know he was there.

He would say
the world is full of secrets.
He would say
listen.

HYDERABAD EVENING

balmy deccan evening
makes it easy to weep

near parched fountains and
crumbling architecture.

where birds dive through
cracked arches and

solitude helps stitch
patches of one's life together.

tears flow with ease as you sit in
secluded courtyard and wonder,

what was this place before the storm?

RIVER MUSI

my beginning lies by the river musi
bisecting my birthplace
between old and new city,
tributary and life source
to a city of pearls.

musi flows like a thin fissure
in a heart now split in two.
polluted river swells and recedes
streaking oily rainbow ripples
over glossy water.

south of the river, old city,
with my father's home and it's shia shrines,
heart and eyes,
memory of floods and
earth that cradles rebellious bones.

north of the river, mallepally,
with my mother's home and it's winding streets,
lungs and gut,
and breath that does not remember
when the sky dips low to kiss you.

on some other earth,
under a different sky,
i dream you.
do you remember me?

your daughter,
born at sunset
a beginning
of evening.

no matter how far,
whatever bridge I cross,
i kneel by your banks,
tenderly cup you in my hands,
love you.

at the river musi,
my city becomes whole.

OVERNIGHT TRAIN

fifteen hour
journey on
a lonely train
through southern india

sloppy urdu
dropping from
a tongue dressed
in a maryland accent

i fall in love with
imaginary places
including the one
i was born

small hands hold
a ticket so thin
holding a translucent wing
of a dragonfly

the sound of tracks
dust and blurred lights
pass like a lullaby
moving in frozen time

PARTITION STORY

I.

My father left this world
and with him some of his story.

I have small bits but
not the whole.

This is the story where we have
returned to Hyderabad together.

Back to the graves of my grandparents.
Back to things that are no longer there.

Maybe he would tell me how much has changed.
Maybe he would tell me what was here once.

The path he walked to school.
The places he loved most.

This was the story I was waiting for.

II.

I cling to glimpses of things
shared quickly over kitchen tables.

Sambar sits in silver bowls
like constellations as he

mentions long walks by cattails,
photographs of reflections in the water,

places he worked, his love of learning.
a determination to save lives.

But I never got
the full story.

It would sit there on the edge
of his lips like a small cloud.

Maybe he left that story on the Deccan plateau.
Maybe he wasn't looking back.

Maybe I never asked.

III.

In a frame is a picture of a small boy
not smiling,

post-partition India,
standing straight

with a heavy bag of books
across his young shoulder like a shield.

Holding in a story—
rain within clouds.

Kept that story
somewhere tucked in

suitcases and train windows,
buses, car rides, planes,

over oceans,
over continents,

Kept it.

IV.

This is the story you will lose
if you do not ask.

AIRPORT PARKING LOT

ebb and flow of
taxis and buses
sigh and release
luggage and laughter as
international flights reunite
fathers with daughters
one continent to another

my watch read 3:55pm and
i knew you had left us

jet planes seared
the sky mute
while windshields of cars
reflected the sun
to clouds of coral
whose every particle
now held you.

ONE HALF HISTORY LOST

aerograms the color of sky
sent from one apartment to
a rented room in another continent

unite years later in a drawer
with the fragrance of
sandalwood and ink.

cornflower tissue thin rivers
contain daffodils and
white pines that touch clouds.

a net carefully woven for years
is cast across the sky—
a dew covered web glistening.

everything weaves back
to homes made
any place on this earth.

across the hemisphere
across salt and blue
clay and dust

i dreamt it real.

MY FATHER'S MRI

In preparation for the test they searched
for a vein to inject dye,
needle to flesh to dehydrated passageways.

I watched the bruising spread
across my skin like blue flowers.
Remembered years before

how they searched you for a vein.
Were you looking up at the ceiling as I did?
Not making eye contact as flowers emerged?

You were fifth in line
to a machine
you would never enter.

At the edge of your skull
by the intersection of infinity,
a silent garden of scarlet bloomed.

I know you felt the weight of me hanging
onto your jacket, our veins eclipsed suns
intertwined under fluorescent lights.

That was me, trying to give
you my spot in line
pushing all of time into a corner,

shoving everything out of the way
that stopped your breath and
pressed you into the sky.

"This will only take
a moment," they said.
I entered a machine.

ALL THE THINGS WE NEVER SAY

are teetering at the edge
frozen by the heart's cliff

a valley of unsent letters
and deleted text messages

they dwell in a parallel dimension
become alternative realities

a easy road veering towards
the direction that was right

a compass in a sea
of synchronicity

a sky full of
clear constellations

the place where
it all worked out.

IMPOSSIBLE

In response to the Muslim Ban

how do you ban soul,
spring, stars,
a butterfly's path,
dense ocean basin currents,
guiding songs of whales,
orbit of moon?

LEDGER

at the morgue during war
is a ledger
thick with soft pages worn
someone maintains it with care
their handwriting precise
ink covering pages
like drops of sapphire
a grieving stream
a weeping sky.

BEFORE BOMBING

it's about to happen

cure to disease
extinguished
answers to questions
hanging

unfinished tea
is still warm
on the table
faint print
of lips
dry on
the edge
of glass

echinacea and
salvias miss
the one that
watered them
bouquets of
sharp trajectories
push into hands
that never wished
to hold them

walls are whispering.

HOW WE WOULD CHANGE

After colonial rule in South Asia,
after partition and
post-colonial realities,
my family immigrated to this land stolen.

Where skyscrapers are
built over burial grounds,
where bodies of resting loved ones
are dug up and put in museums,

displacement even after death.

After emerging under a Deccan sky,
first born daughter
birthed by first born mother,
we came to this land built by kidnapped peoples,

I do not forget.

Five-years-old
and the move felt enormous,
across the world
to an immense parking lot,

the bright lights of
a grocery store
glaring over our
apartment nearby.

REMEMBER THE NIGHT

the police informed us
someone in our neighborhood
did not want us there
our mailbox blown up for the third time

pieces of metal box
falling across the ground
like sharp snowflakes
the year 1979

the year it was common to
blow up mailboxes of people
you want out
of your neighborhood

remember the night the police informed us
someone in our neighborhood
did not want us there
the year 1996

the year our car windows were broken
multiple times in a week
crushed glass under street lights crunching
as they said *not wanted here*

where are we wanted?
where is that place?

i want to be there

PLACE OF BIRTH

i write my place of birth
with attention to

longitude and latitude
planetary alignment

when the earth
on its axis tipped as

the sun set orange on
rocky hyderbadi soil

see the moon rise and
new stars arrange themselves

with care to guide me
in dreams to this place

their light clinging
to untroubled wind

i never lived here
for more than a month

emerged from womb
to this spot

a chasm forever
rewriting itself in my heart

the smoky smell of this air
have I imagined it?

when the longing returns
my eyes reveal visions from

those first days when
the light shined only that way

QURBANI

ma has her hair up with pretty eyeshadow,
salmon chiffon *sari* and *chooriyah*,
dad is in a suit and tie,
my sister and i wear frocks with knee length socks
and the bata shoes because, this is an *event*.

"where are we going ma?" we ask,
"stop asking questions" she says,
the frocks are itchy
and it is hot,
but this is an *event*.

when we finally get to the theater, we are late,
it is filled with the fragrance of aunties and uncles,
perfume and paan, crying babies and chatter,
because who stays quiet in a *filmi* flick?
remember, this is an *event*.

the movie is underway,
a collective gasp overcomes the theater
at the first glance of zeenat aman,
flower in her hair and red sequin dress,
it feels like an *event.*

nazia hassan is singing and
in the dark aisles
of a maryland movie theater
I spin with my sister
at this magnificent *event.*

EID UL-FITR

"hey!" aunty with the silver hair
reflecting the sky,
I haven't seen you in years.
you hug me, whisper in my ear,
"eid mubarak, kid, how have you been?"
I love that you call me *kid* and
feel that way in your embrace.

NIYAZ AT MY MOTHER'S

on a teacup saucer freshly washed raisins
mingle with almonds and cashew,

beads of glistening water
shine like jewels on skin,

the air is filled with the scent
of roses, banana and prayer.

on a humble table line
candles on an aluminum tray,

tiny glowing lights flickering
against the haze of smoke,

agharbati threads twisting
silver braids on fleeting ghosts.

EXPERT

dusty desire to suspend her
in a make-believe past,
traditional
customary
time warp.

instruct her on her plight,
you, ventriloquist voyeur,
telepathic authority
who climbs the bones of her spine
to get a better view.

expert of delusions
speaking of apparitions
draped in black,
non-entities restricted
to fantasy private spaces.

ponder over this *kind* of woman.
grade A, specimen B.
displayed in glass case #5.
scurrying about natural habitat, imaginary woman.
distorted, contorted, shadow woman.

but despite desperate wishes
you can't claim her blood,
healed wounds, heart.
can't explain what you don't know,
indispensable life-force, gut essence, dignity.

unable to contain,
nucleus, incandescent spirit,
who exists
in this modern present,
living   being.

GODDESSES AND DOORMATS

There are only two types of women:
goddesses and doormats. —Pablo Picasso

everyone would like to believe
they are ma'at, venus and kali,
but there are many doormats,
one in front of almost every door.

i feel reverence for the doormat,
beautiful underdog,
unappreciated, disregarded one,
you think isn't anything,
seemingly without gifts and
nothing to say.

in fact, you may not notice her at all.
bristly unassuming thing
with a corny saying on top:

hello

welcome

love

deity at the entrance,
resistant to shock,
immune to damage.
she is the guardian of the doorstep,

the first thing you touch
before entering a home.
perform a daily ritual at her temple
without thinking.

born from the fiber
of tender tissue that
surrounds the seeds of
coconut palms,
the guts of *cocos nucifera*,
made from dignified hands.

people reveal themselves
in her presence.
humble, arrogant, cruel, kind,
she is aware of the manner of the step.

at night, the moon
comes to rest on the small of her back,
craters, scars and light,
her language.

AN EVERYDAY OCCURRENCE

stopped at airport security again
metal detector buzzes conveniently
when I walk through

doesn't matter
that I spent time
to empty pockets of change

remembered not to wear
the belt with the buckle
the metal barrette

pulled to the side
eyes scanning
with suspicion

swabbing and
scouring my body
unwanted touching

stop immediately
for *our* security

like clockwork they peer under hijab
unbutton expose insert prod
pat and feel

when necessary
take to curtained booth and
I must comply

where is *my* security
with arms outstretched
and legs apart

an everyday assault.

STRANGERS ON THE TRAIN

he is the first to notice a
a face gone blank in a
train car of the oblivious

noticed her conversation with a door
closed on half her body and the
slow beginnings of a train picking up speed

she's trying to pull herself in
while he pulls
an emergency stop cord

strangers say i care for you best
because they have
no reason to care

no one knows each other's names
how work was that day
or will i ever speak to you again?

only, "are you ok?"
"yes, thank you"
"see you around"

i see you.

BEGINNING OF SOMETHING

if you swim in the atlantic ocean,
then you know about this.

you know the texture
of the sand, harsh and rough.

the waves, unassuming,
sometimes treacherous.

if you get knocked off your feet,
the ocean here will swallow you.

the shells are sharp and
scrape off skin as you are taken underwater.

submerged in a salty vortex,
your lungs a clenched fist,

the muffled silence
of this other world.

eventually, you are spit to shore,
find yourself in the glaring light,

surrounded by a beach
of people unconcerned.

there is only a little bleeding
under skin torn.

it wasn't a big deal,
a wave,

it took you only for a second,
to that other place.

BLESSED DIVINE WOMAN

Hadrat Fatima Masumah,
your shrine resides
in the middle of this city
like a heart sustaining life,
sanctuary on saline earth,
clear blue solace.

Tonight rose water moistens arid air,
strings of lights shine
like small flowers glowing,
it is the anniversary of your arrival to *Qum*,
You, whose presence
made this city a holy place.

'Aalimah, learned Scholar,
I press my forehead gently
against the entrance to your shrine,
smooth wooden door cools my mind
as I humbly request
your permission to enter.

In the sanctity of this space,
pilgrims' supplications echo against
intricate mirror work above.
Prayers, gratitude and tears blend
like scarlet blue smears of color at dusk,
as our spirits take rest for a moment.

Of the million people who visit your holy grave,
where wishes and hopes
grow like seedling trees,
where we weep as we
request your intercession,
Gracious Healer, we feel heard.

With my heart released in this refuge,
next to other women, their children,
grandmothers with *tasbeh*,
the smell of sweat and roses,
whispers of prayer,
I close my eyes, thankful,

hold this memory of *ziyarat* close,
a salve for wounded days.

SEEING OURSELVES

No matter that I was told to devalue her,
resilient with kaleidoscopic beauty,
flourishing even without nourishment.

Told to embrace apologies for oppression or
pull the frayed edges of fabric
we have woven holding our tale in our words.

How do I see you through the tangled caricature?
Us? Sharing story over dinner as we
carefully weave soul strands together.

Or the serenity of your smile,
as you greet me with peace
on the subway platform.

HYPOTHETICALLY SPEAKING

i place my ear to earth,
listen to the turbulent quiet
of its core.

it tells me this debris filled river
will eventually clear,
dirt will settle

and i will remain,
coolness of moving water
passing around my ankles.

it reminds me to forgive
does not mean to acquiesce,
to give does not mean to evaporate,

to ask for nothing
does not mean
to deserve nothing.

MASOOR DAL

a bag of lentils burst.
masoor dal scattering
across the moving van floor.
at the time she imagined it a blessing.
bright orange path of confetti
welcoming her and her husband
to the new place.

in retrospect, the bag tore,
spilling a haphazard trail
of wasted food
leading to an apartment door,
all swept up later alone,
before she returned
the empty u-haul back
to the garage.

CHANNELING

i wasn't always this way,
worried and unable
to see an end
to multiple storms.

wasn't always this
sad and afraid.
today serves
as a reminder

to years before when i labored,
messy and sweaty,
fantastically filthy,
privately magnificent.

contractions were punctuation marks,
timing was everything,
a kite held with a flick of the wrist
that moves it into a wind current of lift.

"do you need an epidural?" they asked,
"no thank you," i replied,
even though i felt like i was being pressed into earth
by the weight of each band of constricting energy.

split in two but not breaking,
breath intentional,
floating into a rip current,
not moving against it.

OCEAN FIXES EVERYTHING

what happens
here is yours.

MOTH

It isn't in the wings or the flying
where freedom takes place,
it is in the quiet cosmos of
your unbecoming.

In a case of silk
your essence is protected,
while imaginal discs shift,
molt into mystery, cave in.

May a song be an anchor
while your body falls into itself.
May you find beauty
in the reconstruction.

Do you remember
your simultaneous
origin and conclusion?

Do you remember
how once in a cocoon
you met yourself?

BIRTH

fingers from my left hand trace letters in the earth,
my right floating in and out of cloud.
it is your name on my lips, child,
in this space between known and unknown.

splitting apart skin, stretched thin and burning,
body purging everything moments before you arrive.
releasing wounds like birds free,
body tired from holding so long.

you wait for this to happen, then, descend,
my pelvis aching as you depart.
womb shrinking goodbye
in deep sighs.

FINDING HOME

In this room filled with late night dreaming,
your cries wake me again.

Is it the fifth time you woke?
Is it really 5:00 am?

The scent of you, fresh and safe,
skin soft, moonlight's caress on moving water.

The four-days-old of you,
bundled close against me.

Was it you inside me all along?
You within me?

When I learned of your presence,
summer's gentleness against my skin,

the air gleamed bright,
sky clear, open.

In my muscular nest you nuzzled,
swam in a concealed sea,

urgently grew,
beneath my heart.

You are here now,
drinking breast milk

in the last sigh of this night,
fragile life in my care.

I curl around you fatigued,
feeling some ancient story

coursing through me,
your warm breath

painting luminescent landscapes
against my skin.

At this moment she swept over me,
home did. Not the brick variety or nation.

Though I searched for her,
it was she who found me.

We wept in the serene yellow
light glowing sincere,

exchanged stories, reconciled.
She missed me.

Was this me? Bearer of life,
birthing dreams

under the light of the last stars
shining before daybreak,

nourishing and protecting my now sleeping infant
fluttering smiles of contentment like sunlight,

my own belly full of belonging,
after finding myself.

HEAVEN LIES AT THE FEET

these are the words of 3am cleaning the sheets
after you threw up for the third time tonight.

these words are the ones that will do anything for you
tie your shoes a million times if you asked.

the words that gladly wait the extra hour
at the table while you play with your food.

the words that answer all of your questions,
no matter how many.

these are the words who sang to you before you were born,
stayed awake with you, humbled.

these words want to show you the beauty of this world,
discover new things, strive for justice.

these words wash your clothes and pack your lunches,
drop you to school.

these words do homework with you,
read stories.

these words are not glamorous,
they smell of sweat, salt and *haldi*.

these words aren't asking
for anything in return,

they want to give you
everything.

MERI JAAN

child, you arrived in the summer,
cool salty *lassi* afternoon in the poetry

lingering in old bollywood theaters in queens
and coltrane in the evening.

you arrived in happy times where i gave of
myself to others and to myself.

you come from sea, air and light,
pure earth, sweat and love.

you picked this time to be.
how could i forget this?

we are here when we
are supposed to be and

i remember who i am.

LEFT BREAST

the room was dark
but for the gleam of
your image.

aglow from the inside
a constellation
in velvet space.

your bluish light
floating off the screen,
translucent jellyfish.

how many times have
I cupped you in my hand?
you're over my heart.

the day my son was born
I understood you more.
how his mouth reached,

a small bird with eyes closed
drawn to a voice
that insisted, live.

I felt your burn and creation,
dormant volcano
gone active.

never knew what you were
capable of, and maybe
I still do not know.

I stand before a map
in reverence.
ultra-violet distributary

diverting off
a main channel,
then rejoining.

I am seeing you
from the inside
for the first time.

BETWEEN YOU AND YOU

somewhere on a cliff
in the himalayas
you smelled the fragrance
of your own mortality.
found your reflection
in the mud.

honored the way you loved.
the way your heart broke.
how life became living.
became generative,
regenerative magic.
mimicked nature.
experienced itself.

when the boulders lodged
in your spine finally turned to dust,
when you learned
how to stand straight,
when you laid flowers
at the entrance to your womb,
when a thread of light
lit a river through you,
a conduit between
earth's core and infinity,

here, you kissed the middle
of your own palm,
above the life line
below the heart line.
experienced how spirit
rests in colors at the edge of breath,
meridians small portals to
no space or time.

stopped longing,
wishing, caring,
became bone, blood, breath,
a heart of four chambers,
in release.

NOTES

The book's epigraph is from Agha Shahid Ali's, *Land*.

Ayatul Kursi is the 255th verse of the 2nd surah of the Qur'an, *Al-Baqara*.

´*Alif Lām Mīm* are sacred untranslatable letters found in the opening verses of certain surahs in the Qur'an.

The title *Qurbani* (English: *Sacrifice*) is from a 1980's Hindi film starring Zeenat Aman. The film is known for the song *Aap Jaisa Koi* sung by Pakistani singer, Nazia Hassan.

The title *Heaven Lies at the Feet* is inspired from a Hadith (narration) where the Prophet Muhammad (PBUH) has said: *Heaven lies at the feet of the mother.*

ACKNOWLEDGEMENTS

Thank you to the editors of the following publications, where earlier versions of these poems first appeared:

- **Hyderabad Evening**
  Salt Journal and *Roots & Culture Magazine*
- **Airport Parking Lot**
  Mizna Journal, Volume 10
- **My Father's MRI**
  Apiary Magazine, Volume 6
- **Impossible**
  Origins Journal, UnMargin
- **Ledger**
  Mizna Journal, Volume 8
- **Before Bombing**
  Stop Being Famous
- **Place of Birth**
  A View From the LOFT
- **Expert**
  Shattering the Stereotypes: Muslim Women Speak Out (Olive Branch Press); *Mizna Journal*, Volume 3 and *A View From the LOFT*
- **Strangers on The Train**
  Dusie, Issue 19

- **Blessed Divine Woman**
  Living Islam Out Loud: American Muslim Women Speak (Beacon Press)

- **Seeing Ourselves**
  Shattering the Stereotypes: Muslim Women Speak Out (Olive Branch Press) and *A View From the LOFT*

- **Finding Home**
  Living Islam Out Loud: American Muslim Women Speak (Beacon Press)

- **Birth**
  Mizna Journal, Volume 10

I am grateful to Upset Press for their ceaseless faith and belief. Thank you to my dear friends, mentors and editors for your unending generosity, encouragement and care.
This book would not exist without you.

Thank you to my family in this world and the hereafter.

To my son, my love and inspiration, thank you.